# The Ultimate 101 Facebook User Guide

*by Neo Monefa*

# Table of Contents

# 1. Introduction

If you gather all the Facebook users in the world, you could build a country of 943 million people— that's about three times the population of the United States. Each day, hundreds of millions of people across the globe log on to their Facebook pages with the average person spending hours surfing, posting content, and interacting in the virtual community. What Facebook has been able to achieve in this generation was totally unimaginable decades ago; it has revolutionized the way people interact and communicate.

Who doesn't know Facebook? Who doesn't have a Facebook account? Even in some of the smallest countries where the use of computer is almost non-existent, the locals are familiar with the term 'Facebook'. Even our parents who never really showed interest in anything techy, are now on Facebook. It has become the language of interaction and communication today. We hear people say, 'I'll talk to you on Facebook' or 'Check out my Facebook page for updates'; it's easy, it's free, and it's open to all!

In this fast-paced generation, Facebook allows people to interact and keep in touch with just a few clicks on the computer or their smart phone. It is the fastest, most convenient way to stay in touch with your network of friends. And speaking of network, Facebook allows users to build an entire network of friends – sky's the limit! And since everyone's on it, you can find all your friends here; it's the best place to rekindle with your high school classmates or those long lost relatives—add them up and you'll be catching up with them in no time.

One of the best things about Facebook is it allows you to share a part of yourself to others. It's like this virtual album that's open to all your friends. For most users, it also serves as their interactive diary where they keep a journal of the important events in their lives with photos, videos, and even blogs. It allows the virtual community to share a slice of your life, and invites your network of friends to be a part of every milestone in your journey. It is by far the best thing that has happened in the online world.

With the rise of Facebook over the recent years, came to popularity topics like social media, Twitter, and blogging—in today's generation, who doesn't know these terms? Millions spend hours each day on the Internet doing exactly these things—Facebooking, tweeting, and blogging! As a result, many new phrases have been coined such as 'like my photo', 'add me', 'tag me'… and so many more. But the amazing thing is, if you're anywhere near this generation then you definitely know and even use these phrases often.

There's no denying how much Facebook has revolutionized the way people interact and share information. There's absolutely nothing like Facebook today, and it may take a long while before something like it comes around.

# 2. The Story Behind Facebook: The Rise to Success

The recent movie 'Social Network' captures the story behind the multi-million dollar idea that built what we now all know as Facebook. You guessed it right, like most brilliant discoveries it all started with a simple yet great idea that was carried though to success. Facebook's rise to success was not without challenge. Its founder Mark Zuckerberg had to face law suits and countless accusations in his journey to the top. The real story behind Facebook has been under dispute since day one; with so many controversies surrounding the people involved with building it. But the 19-year-old Harvard sophomore was unstoppable, since he launched then called 'thefacebook.com' the site had nowhere to go but up. It was an instant hit among the Harvard students and surrounding colleges and universities, and word about it quickly spread like wild fire, and as they say everything was history.

Today, Facebook is one of the most visited and most widely known sites in the entire world! Zuckerberg's success story is much like a well-written script from a movie, complete with exciting twists and an unbelievable climax.

Here's a quick look on the highlights surrounding the creation of Facebook and the key events that have been plagued by controversies. The very week Facebook was launched its creator Mark Zuckerberg was accused of stealing the idea from three Harvard students, so how did he still manage to pull through with it and make history? Did he really steal the idea?

Though legal settlements have been made between parties involved, the real score still remains debatable depending on whose side of the story you hear it from. Please note that some information here may not be authenticated by Zuckerberg or Facebook but it's worth the read so you can decide for yourself.

Facemash

In October 2003, sophomore Mark Zuckerberg while at his dorm room at Harvard had an idea to create his own version of the popular site Hot or Not; he wanted something exclusive to Harvard students. And so he came up with Facemash.

The idea was simple—he took two photos of students and placed them side-by-side trying to compare who has hot and who was not; students voted who they thought were more attractive. The thing is Zuckerberg had to hack into the private Harvard student directory to be able to obtain students' photos. Amazingly, Facemash was a hit among the students. In just two weeks, over 400 students were recorded to have visited the site, garnering some 22,000 votes!

Zuckerberg was a 'celebrity' overnight. He was now known in campus as the one who built Facemash. But the site was short lived; after being called by the school's disciplinary board and threatened to be expelled, the site was immediately shut down. He faced sanctions for breach of school security, copyrights violation, and violating student privacy for stealing their photos and using it publicly. Zuckerberg faced expulsion; luckily all his sanctions were dropped and he was allowed to continue in Harvard.

HarvardConnections.com

In the same year, three Harvard seniors Tyler Winklevoss, Cameron Winklevoss, and Divya Narendra were looking for a reliable web developer to create a social media site. The three students had been sitting on the idea for some time and needed someone to help them get it running. The three had initially worked with a certain Victor Gao who soon begged off the project and recommended Zuckerberg as his replacement.

After the Facemash incident that went public around Harvard, Zuckerberg was now a name associated with creating amazingly popular websites. As expected, the three agreed to have him as replacement.

Tyler Winklevoss, Cameron Winklevoss, and Divya Narendra wanted to create a social network site designed for Harvard students and alumni; the site was to be called HarvardConnections.com. The long term plan was to eventually expand the social network site to other colleges and universities.

Zuckerberg was excited about the idea after the three met with him to share their vision for HarvardConnections.com. He agreed to help them set-up and launch the site. He writes in two succeeding emails to the three:

"I read over all the stuff you sent and it seems like it shouldn't take too long to implement, so we can talk about that after I get all the basic functionality up tomorrow night."

"I put together one of the two registration pages so I have everything working on my system now. I'll keep you posted as I patch stuff up and it starts to become completely functional."

It was all supposed to go as planned until the controversial twist happened. Tyler Winklevoss, Cameron Winklevoss, and Divya Narendra soon alleged that Zuckerberg, after only a few email exchanges about the project, suddenly began to purposely delay the development of their site because he had actually stolen their idea and was creating something similar to it. Zuckerberg allegedly never really intended to finish HarvardConnections.com as he feared it would compete with the site he was about to launch—the one they say was based on the idea he stole from them.

From being enthusiastic about it, Zuckerberg began to give all sorts of excuses for not being able to deliver on his word. According to the three, this was about the same time he was working on his own site using their idea. He writes in an email to the three:

"The week has been pretty busy thus far, so I haven't gotten a chance to do much work on the site or even think about it really, so I think it's probably best to postpone meeting until we have more to discuss. I'm also really busy tomorrow so I don't think I'd be able to meet then anyway."

Though these emails were all made public during the trials, Zuckerberg ofcourse never validated these allegations. He stands by his argument that there was never any breach of contract or intellectual rights. As mentioned in one of the legal trials, there was no clear contract or agreement entered by both parties during the entire process of their dealings aside from 'dorm room chit-chats'. And Zuckerberg stands by that. He created something no one else could, and there is no fault in that.

Weeks passed and he never got to complete the project with the three. Instead, he soon launched what he never thought would make history—'thefacebook.com'.

At the end of all the arguments and controversies, whether it was a stolen idea or not really doesn't matter anymore. More than 900 million people worldwide think it's the coolest thing today! And that says it all.

On February 4, 2004, Zuckerberg launched his site thefacebook.com initially open only to Harvard students. That same summer, he started working on the site full time. Not long after, what started as Harvard social network site grew the interest of other colleges and universities in the country, until it started spreading like wild fire all over the globe to become one of the biggest global enterprise today.

In the first 30 days of its launch, thefacebook.com had over half of the Harvard undergraduates signing up in the site. By this time, Zuckerberg had commissioned the help of his friends to develop the site; he brought in Andrew McCollum, Dustin Moskovitz, and Eduardo Saverin.

Until June 2004, Facebook was known as thefacebook. The succeeding year, Zuckerberg decided to drop the 'the' creating its new name Facebook.

There was now no stopping the growth and spread of Facebook. High school students were the next biggest users before it was publicly available to anyone 13 years old and above. Not long after, everyone was on it—teenagers, parents, businesses, political groups, fan clubs, and even children and the elderly. There were no limitations to who could enjoy the social networking world.

Today, there is still nothing like it. It is one of the most visited sites of this generation, with millions of people logging on every single day. It is the best way to interact with people, hook up with friends, send updates about yourself to the world, and just stay connected with the social networking world.

No matter all the allegations and controversies, Mark Zuckerberg will continue to be an inspiration to the world for creating something that revolutionized this generation. One thing that can't be disputed is the phenomenal success of his creation.

In a statement issued by Zuckerberg and Facebook regarding these law suits, it reads: "We're not going to debate the disgruntled litigants and anonymous sources who seek to rewrite Facebook's early history or embarrass Mark Zuckerberg with dated allegations. The unquestioned fact is that since leaving Harvard for Silicon Valley nearly six years ago, Mark has led Facebook's growth from a college website to a global service playing an important role in the lives of over 400 million people."

## The People Behind Facebook

Whenever discussions about the history and beginning of Facebook is made, it is inevitable to include some important names who play a part in the story. There are people who will forever be stuck with the story of Facebook; and their contributions whether big or small played a part in the entire story.

Let's take a look at these people and find out where they are now.

### Mark Zuckerberg

His name is synonymous to the creation of the biggest social networking site Facebook. He is now the chairman and chief executive of Facebook Inc.

Since the unstoppable success of Facebook, in 2010 he was identified by Time Magazine to be among the 100 richest and most influential people in the entire world.

### Eduardo Saverin

Saverin is co-founder of Facebook working with Zuckerberg during their college years in Harvard. In 2004, after its launch, he held the position of chief financial officer. However, as Facebook continued to expand the Saverin and Zuckerberg began having conflicts regarding its business direction. This resulted in Saverin's diminished involvement in running the business.

He later a filled a lawsuit against Facebook and Zuckerberg for the alleged unlawful dilution of his shares in Facebook. The charges have been settled out of court.

## Sean Parker

Though nothing was mentioned in the history about this character, Sean Parker played a role in the development of Facebook during its early years. Being an American entrepreneur and co-founder of the popular music file sharing Napster, Sean Parker had great insights to share with Zuckerberg after the initial launch of the Facebook. Also, having had an experience as an advisor to the Friendster founder, Sean became the first president of Facebook. To this day, his contributions are greatly valued by the site.

## Tyler Winklevoss, Cameron Winklevoss, and Divya Narendra

When you talk about the founding days of Facebook it's impossible not to mention these personalities. In the recent movie depiction of how Facebook was founded, these three names became widely famous. Tyler and Cameron were both part of the Harvard rowing team back in college.

The law suit these three filed were reportedly ended with a $65 million dollars settlement. The three were recently spotted creating SumZero a social network specifically for professional investors.

# 3. Interesting Facebook Trivia

The story behind Facebook is like one written for a movie; from the controversies, exciting twists, law suits, and then its phenomenal success. When Facebook became public there were other social networking sites that came before it, but it just took the world by storm and before anybody knew we were all on Facebook exchanging photos, sharing conversations, and liking each other's posts. In a few years' time, Facebook users went from a few hundred thousand to hundreds of millions. To date, only a few millions more and Facebook would hit the 1 billion mark!

There's obviously no stopping the popularity of Facebook worldwide. Social network just gets better and bigger by the day, and Facebook undeniably wants to stay ahead of the pack with new innovations and more creative ideas. And the public can't seem to get enough of Facebook's success story and how a single idea went from a Harvard dorm room to become a billion dollar enterprise. No matter the controversies behind Mark Zuckerberg, his story remains to be an inspiration and a role model to millions of people across the world.

Aside from the story of how Facebook was created, there are also some very interesting bits and pieces of information worth finding out. Below are a few quick information and trivia you may never have known until now.

• Trivia 1. There are currently an estimated 955 million Facebook users across 211 countries. That's about three times the population of the United States. If you were to put all of them in one place, then we could have a Facebook country.

• Trivia 2. The following are the top 5 Facebook nations in the world ranked by the most number of users:
1. United States – 166 million

2.      Brazil – 58 million
3.      India – 56 million
4.      Indonesia – 43 million
5.      United Kingdom – 42 million

•       Trivia 3. In the US alone, Facebook accounted for 400 billion of all page views on the internet this year; that's 1.6 billion a week or around 229 million Facebook views a day!

•       Trivia 4. The average time a person spends on Facebook is about 20 minutes. But others can spend hours on end surfing the social media world.

•       Trivia 5. More than half of all Facebook visits come from only 10 US states, including California, New York, Texas, Pennsylvania, Illinois, Georgia, Ohio, North Carolina, and Michigan. This is how much Americans love Facebook.

•       Trivia 6. Aside from the US, Facebook is also the top website in the following countries: Singapore, Canada, New Zealand, and Hong Kong. This is the amazing effect of Facebook to the entire world.

•       Trivia 7. 56% of all recorded Facebook users are female. There seems to be no clear explanation why women love Facebook more than men.

•       Trivia 8. Facebook landed the spot as the most searched word in the US for three years since 2009. This shouldn't be so surprising considering its over 900 million users and counting.

•       Trivia 9. There are close to 1 billion photos uploaded to Facebook each month! That's how much people love sharing photos. How many photos do you post on Facebook in a week?

- Trivia 10. Over 30 million Facebook users update their status message at least once each day with whatever they feel like writing. Freedom of expression is one of the best things users enjoy with Facebook—you can write what you want... as long as you don't offend other people.

- Trivia 11. Mark Zuckerberg the founder of Facebook is the world's youngest billionaire! This is how far he has taken that dorm room idea. From a simple project to a billion dollar estate!

- Trivia 12. Mark Zuckerberg appeared in business investment meetings at Wall Street wearing a hoodie side by side with business men in thousand dollar suits. But for someone who discovered a billion dollar enterprise he could get away with wearing anything!

- Trivia 13. The number of photos and videos uploaded on Facebook last year by its over 900 million users is said to be double all existing written works of all people across the world. This is how much people love sharing and posting stuff!

- Trivia 14. Mark Zuckerberg's 28% share of Facebook makes him worth over $29 billion! He's the only living person that age who amounts this much.

- Trivia 15. If you make Facebook into a nation, it would land the third largest spot—behind China and India.

# 4. Getting Started with Facebook

After reading the interesting story behind this generation's greatest creation, then you need to jump right on and het started! If you're not yet on Facebook then you're missing what over 900 million people are enjoying every single day. Or if you are already on Facebook but don't seem to be enjoying it all that much, then you may not be maximizing the power of this tool. Find out what you may be missing out on, and start loving social media!

**Why do People Love Facebook?**

The answers to this question could be endless. There are over 900 million people signed up with an account on Facebook, over 400 million of which are active users. All of them may have their own reason for loving this social networking site.

Whether you're on Facebook for business or just plain leisure and fun, you definitely have your own unique reason for loving Facebook. Go over these common reasons why people just love this networking site. You, why do you love Facebook?

• It brings family and loved ones closer to home. You get to stay in touch with friends and family in an instant. No matter how far away they live, Facebook brings them closer to home!

• It gives you a chance to reconnect with people you have never seen or heard from in years! Find college friends and even high school teachers on Facebook... they're all there.

- Now, there's no need to send mail or greeting cards to relatives overseas, because Facebook will keep you in touch with them instantly and for free. There are even e-greetings cards you can send through Facebook. How cool is that?

- You can share pictures with your network of close friends or choose to share it to the entire world! You can create albums to document important events in your life and share it with others.

- After enjoying your friends' photos you can leave meaningful notes on them and start really fun virtual conversations. Click 'like' to express your appreciation on a certain photo.

- It's one of the best ways to meet new people and interact with them. There's no limit to the people you can find and meet over social media. Add new people as friends and get to build new acquaintances.

- There are tons of games and really cool apps to keep you entertained. If you're into Internet games then you would definitely find Facebook's games a hit. Depending on your age and interest, there's a game that will suit you.

- Learning is never ending! With all the information and news shared by millions of people you get to learn something new every time you're on Facebook. The topics are also limitless, people can talk about anything under the sun—fashion, current events, sports, movies, science... name it!

- It's the best way to stay connected with the world! Don't stay hidden under that rock, connect with the world around you and learn the things that are happening around.

- It's a great source of up to date news about what's happening around you. When something happens, Facebook immediately carries headlines about it. Their news is fast and reliable.

- With Facebook, users enjoy their freedom of expression. They can post what they want and interact with who they want to. Of course, users are always encouraged to be responsible with their content and behavior over social media.

- No matter how far your friends are, you get to interact with them as if they were just next door. Time and distance really don't matter when you're on Facebook. You can chat with them, share photos and videos and just enjoy your virtual connection.

- Through a Facebook page your business can get all the marketing and promotion for free! Businesses have found Facebook Pages the best and most cost efficient way to sell their products and services. With over 400 million people actively using Facebook, it's the best marketing tool.

- It's the fastest way to communicate and interact with customers and clients.

Great customer service has never been as easy with Facebook. Business owners can respond to client concerns immediately; they can even exchange real time virtual conversations.

- You get to stay updated on what's in and what's not. Facebook is a great resource for the latest in fashion, music, movies, and entertainment.

**Creating a Facebook Account**

Just the fact that you're interested with this e-book you probably already have a Facebook account. And if you're not living under a rock or something, then you definitely have some working knowledge of the internet and Facebook; if you think about it we can totally skip this part. But just to complete this e-book, here's a quick guide on how to create a Facebook account.

Now that you're pretty impressed at how Facebook was created and how it has revolutionized the world, then it would be a shame not to jump into the bandwagon and see it for yourself. Now, you already have an existing account then you might want to try creating a second account.

Go through these no-brainer steps and you'll have a Facebook account working in no time.

**STEP 1:**

Go to Facebook.com to begin signing up for an account. You will see a sign up form you need to fill out with important information. Don't worry, Facebook is one of the most user friendly sites today, so signing up will definitely be a breeze.

Make sure you input accurate and correct information. Once you're done, hit Sign Up to complete the initial process.

**STEP 2:**

After clicking Sign Up, you will see a three-step process that will help you completely set up your account. Don't forget to click Save at the end of each step. Or you can choose to temporarily skip a step and return to it when you're ready.

The first step is to invite friends into your social network. Facebook offers ways on how best to find friends; you can directly input their email address, search them over Skype, and other email services. Then, you can move on to fill out important personal information about yourself. This will help your friends and the social networking world get to know you.

Lastly, you will have the chance to upload your profile picture. You can upload an existing photo or take a new one through your web cam.

**STEP 3:**

That's it! Your Facebook account is now ready! Don't worry if your account looks empty, uploading content, and customizing your account is just as easy. Now that you have an account you can be as creative and fun as possible with it. You can also edit the photo and other information you have initially uploaded.

Welcome to your very own Facebook account!

**How to find Friends on Facebook**

Now that you're Facebook account is up and ready, there's one thing you should get right on—inviting and adding friends!

The whole idea of social media is networking with the virtual community across the world. Facebook will help you find friends you haven't heard from in years, or family members living abroad whom you haven't seen in a while, you can even meet new friends in the social community.

The more friends you are able to connect with and the bigger your network of friends is the more fun your Facebook experience is! Share photos, videos, and stories with your friends every time you're logged in your account—it's free, convenient, and so much fun!

Everything about Facebook is so user friendly, but just to make sure you get to connect with as many of your friends as possible here are some very useful tips to help you.

Facebook provides three easy steps for users to search and invite their friends:

### 1. Search for Friends

You can simply type the name of a friend you are looking for at the Search bar at the top of the page. If nothing comes up then try refining and filtering your search further. Use the dropdown tabs to filter your search either by location, education background, or workplace. You will be surprised how many people you know are already on Facebook, and they will be thrilled to see you!

### 2. Import your Contacts

If you have all your contacts stored in your email don't worry because Facebook will help you import all these to invite them to connect with you through Facebook. Go the Find Friends tab and input the account from which you would like to import contacts. Once you have successfully imported your contacts, Facebook will give you the option to automatically send an invite to those already in Facebook. It's that easy!

### 3. Invite Friends Individually

You also have the option of inviting people individually through the Invite Your Friends tab. All you need to do is to input their email address and a simple message for them and hit Invite! A Facebook invitation will automatically be sent to your personal friends.

In the same way, you will be surprised how many people will add you up to their Facebook network. Once your name is searchable on Facebook all your old time friends can easily spot you. Expect invites after invites to arrive at your Facebook inbox! This is now your opportunity to hook up with high school classmates, college professors, and those long lost relatives. Once a college batch mate finds you, word will get around the social networking world and many others will soon find you. Try searching for new people every once in a while, you'll never know who you might suddenly spot. That's the amazing thing about Facebook! It connects you to the entire virtual world!

**How to Write Interesting Facebook Updates**

Now that you have all your friends connected with it's time to make your Facebook as interesting as possible. The best part of your Facebook experience is uploading content and sharing it with your network. And It gets even more exciting when interesting conversations are generated from a single post you make. Obviously, people are more compelled to start conversation threads from more engaging content... but boring posts will definitely be ignored.

Remember that your Facebook account and all the content you post mirror the kind of person you are and the stuff you are interested in... so if you don't want to be branded as boring and un-cool then try to post and share stuff that are timely, exciting, and meaningful to you friends. Just keep it real and have fun! Don't try to project somebody you're not.

Here are a few useful tips on how to upload and share content that your friends will most likely find interesting and will have a higher chance of creating long threads of comments.

- **Short is the way to go.** Never post lengthy, dragging messages. People on Facebook and the internet for that matter do not stop to read long writings, they just browse through pages and stop at posts and content they find engaging and interesting enough. Study shows that posts around 40 characters get 86% higher chances of engaging people.

- **Keep things simple.** Nobody wants to study a science experiment on Facebook, so try to upload simple content that's easy to relate to. You can upload photos, videos, and even links to your blog.

- **Questions are naturally more engaging.** Try to ask direct and interesting questions to capture people's attention at a glance. Those who are more inclined to share an advice or air their comment will most likely respond and get the conversation rolling.

- **Use visuals.** Nothing works better to capture people's attention than great photos. As they say 'a picture paints a thousand words'. What would take an entire article to explain may be easily captured in a single photo. So if made to choose between an article post or a photo, go for visuals.

- **Mix it up.** Stop posting the same thing over and over especially if no one really interacts and responds to it. Try to give your posts a creative mix—try videos, polls, photos, or at times just a simple one-liner post could create a storm of responses when done right. Don't just post personal stuff that's all about yourself, mix it up with current events, exciting events, inspirational quotes... just try to have fun with it.

- **Be responsive.** When someone asks you something don't just ignore them, respond to their requests or their questions—after all, this is what Facebook was created for: to interact with people in the social network. Try to acknowledge people's comments, questions, and requests.

- **When writing, use simple conversational language.** Write as if you are talking to someone face to face. Remember people go to Facebook to exchange fun conversations and interactions and not to read boring stuff. Don't lecture when you write, just simply share an idea.

## Important Facebook Terms

While you explore the world of Facebook and social media you are bound to bump into a million terms that may not sound all too familiar. These terminologies will help you better navigate your way through social media and allow you to have so much more fun while you're at it! Yes, there's so much more to Facebook than you know... there are countless ways to have fun with this tool than you can imagine.

Okay, so before you go on with your Facebook journey, go over these important terms and make suer you're familiar with them.

- **Social Media.** This may refer entirely to the use of internet, web surfing, and connecting with people through the virtual social networks.

- **Apps.** This is short for the word 'application' an refers to separate services that can help you make the most out of your Facebook use.

- **Events.** Facebook allows you to create events straight from your account and invite people from your contacts. You can indicate all the important information about your event and even have your rsvp right from the site.

• **Groups.** These are specific communities that share a specific interest. You can create your own Facebook Group and invite specific people whom you think will best fit the group. Groups can be cause-related, it can be a fan club, or a high school graduating batch… it's up you.

• **Insights.** These are the analytics provided by Facebook to help users evaluate how their page is performing.

• **Message.** Facebook users can share private, direct messages much like an email.

• **Like.** This is the thumbs up icon you see right next to every Facebook post. Simply click on it to show your appreciation on a specific content, a photo, or video.

• **Notification.** This is the list of all updates you receive from your friends and contacts and the pages you liked since your last log in. This will help you keep up with the activities going on in your social community.

• **Cover Photo.** This is the big photo that appears right smack at the center of your Facebook Page. This photo ay be replaced from time to time to give your page a fresh look.

• **Profile Picture.** Different from you cover photo, the profile picture is the thumbnail photo that appears in front of the cover photo. This is also the photo that appears every time you post content or make a comment on someone else's page.

- **Status.** This may refer to the updates and content you share and post on your wall. You can also share what's on your mind as your status for your friends to see.

- **Info Tab.** This allows you to update and edit information about you, your group, or your business.

- **Wall.** This is where the most exciting interactions take place. This is where you post updates and status messages that will engage your friends into conversation threads.

- **Twitter.** Much like Facebook, Twitter is also a social networking tool that allows people to stay connected and interactive through short messages called 'tweets'.

- **Blog.** A blog is like a person's online journal. Remember your diary days? It's the same thing except that it's online.

- **Viral Marketing.** This is classified as a marketing technique designed to spread information like a 'virus' across the virtual world. Viral materials may be in the form of videos, photos, or blogs.

- **Email Marketing.** This is another marketing technique wherein information about a product or service is disseminated through email.

- **Google.** This is today's premiere and most used search engine. It is so widely used that a verb has already been coined from it, people today say 'Google it' to refer the act of searching something on the Internet.

# 5. Having Fun on Facebook

The entire purpose of you being on Facebook is to have fun! Whether you're connecting with friends, sharing stuff to the world, or selling your business... it should all be really fun! Facebook was designed to allow users to express themselves while connecting to the world and customize and create their own Facebook experiences. Yes, at Facebook you're the boss... you get to decide how to go about socializing in the virtual community and what apps and services to use.

So now that you have your own account ready and have invited your friends, it's time to have more fun with it!

**Having Fun with Facebook Apps**

Using applications is one of the best ways to have fun while on Facebook. There are tons of apps out there, from games, quizzes, design tools, and so many other helpful stuff to add excitement to your experience. The best part is most apps are downloadable for free! So you can download them, use them, and delete them when you find a better app.

If you're looking for a tool to help you manage your content, then there are apps for video, photo, and blog management that will help you post and share more conveniently. If you're looking for tools to make your Facebook account more colorful and creative, then go ahead and download design apps that will give life to your Facebook Page! Whatever your need is, there's an app that's right for you. Don't be scare to mess up your page, you won't. These apps are so easy to use and navigate.

But since there are thousands of apps out there, here are a few of the most useful and widely downloaded apps that you can try.

## 1. HootSuite

With the rise in popularity of social network and the internet, so many channels are now available to connect to people and market your business. Some years ago, users had to repost their content repeatedly if they wanted a similar content posted across their various social network channels. But with the creation of HootSuite users can now have the convenience of managing their content through a central hub—Facebook. Now, when you post something on Facebook, HootSuite helps you post the same on Twitter, MySpace, LinkedIn, YouTube and other sites.

## 2. iFrames

Your Facebook Page will never be the same once you try Wildfire's iFrames. Goodbye to that boring Facebook look with this app that will dress up your site like never before. Capture more attention on your site with cool iFrames. You'll be surprised how much likes you'll get after downloading and trying out this app.

## 3. Pagemodo

If you're looking for professionally done business page templates then Pagemodo is the app to get. Customize our welcome page with interesting videos, eye-catching photos, and text using this app. You can also easily create a fan gate to spice up your Facebook Page. And for added convenience, Pagemodo allows you to sync feeds from your Twitter straight to your Facebook account. If you're looking to have fun designing your Facebook site, then you need to try out this app.

## 4. Facebook Polls

This free app allows you to get all your friends talking about your posts and answering your poll questions. It's one of the best ways to keep your friends engaged and having fun! Just type in whatever question you want, leave a few options for them to rank, and that's it… you'll be surprised at how many of your friends will be joining in the polls. Business pages also find this app a great tool to engage their customers and get them to answer questions about their product and services.

**5. Woobox**

This app will allow businesses to give out coupons to their fans. Electronic coupons can easily be generated and given to users as prizes and freebies. It's a sure way to generate traffic and even product sales.

There are so many other apps out there that will allow you to create so much more on your Facebook site. To help you go over different applications more conveniently, go to your Facebook account's search tab and key in the app 'Search Apps'. Download this app to assist you in looking for other useful applications. Browse through thousands of other entertaining and useful apps with Search Apps. *Refer to screenshot below.*

**Be a Responsible Facebook User**

While having fun with Facebook and enjoying the interaction you have with the virtual community, you need to keep in mind that there are so many other people using Facebook and social media— that's over 900 million people on Facebook alone. With this in mind, you need to be careful with the information you exchange and also be sensitive to others around you. It's fine to have the freedom to post stuff and make comments, but remember not to use that freedom to step on others. And since you don't really know everyone on the social network you need to be careful with the information and materials you share and even the people you interact with.

Below are some quick reminders on how to use Facebook more responsibly and the things you should avoid, in this way you can have so much more fun with it while staying safe.

- When you're hesitant to share content that is otherwise private, then don't post it or share it through Facebook. There are other more secure and private ways to do so.

- Customize your Facebook account's privacy settings. But don't just rely on it, practice safety.

- Practically whatever communication you post through Facebook stays forever. So be very careful with the comments and communication threads you make.

- Facebook does not support irresponsible use of the site, such as posting content that is offensive to others, posts that threaten or harass, content that uses abusive language, and anything that is racially or ethnically offensive. The site is for connecting with people in a positive manner and not a platform for attacking people.

- Never put your personal information like contact numbers in publicly shared comment threads to other people's post.

- As much as possible, confirm only the invitation of people you know. Just try to quickly double check if you have friends in common that may confirm the person's background. Also, never add people you don't know.

- Never stalk people on Facebook. Don't make phony accounts just so you can try to add people without them knowing who you are. Never pretend to be someone else just to get the attention of certain people.

•       Be respectful of others while having fun on Facebook. Do not post photos or videos of people without their consent. Never borrow content written by other people without acknowledging them. It's fine to repost or use good stuff from others, but you need to properly acknowledge the real author.

•       Children 13 years old and below is advised to seek parental consent before signing up an account on Facebook. Parents should guide their children through the sign up process to ensure proper information.

•       Children's use of Facebook must be supervised. So much random content is shared over social media that may not be suitable for children. And it would be impossible to filter stuff on the net.

•       Stay away from cyber bullying. When people start picking on someone else on social network this is called cyber bullying; do not play a role in any of this. Facebook is created for people to have fun with and enjoy, so let's keep it that way.

•       Do not turn to Facebook as an outlet to broadcast your problems. It's fine to post status messages about your concerns, but to go into detail in a public channel such as Facebook might be damaging to you in the future. Share it only with your closest peers.

•       Proofread your status message before hitting the enter key. Nobody wants to read ill-written posts. And you sure don't want to be branded as trying hard. And, really, nobody wants to hear a blow by blow account of your entire day written on your status. There tons of other stuff to write about, it doesn't always have to be about yourself.

•       Remind yourself that you don't live to surf Facebook. Allot a specific time each day for social media surfing and never miss out on other important activities such as studying, going to work on time, spending time with family, and even eating on time. Be responsible with managing your time with Facebook.

# 6. Facebook and Your Business

In this techy generation, almost everyone is on social media. Millions from across the world access and spend hours on social media everyday-- whether for leisure, entertainment, or business purposes.

Have you ever stopped to imagine how with a quick Facebook post thousands and even millions of people can readily see it and connect with you? That's how powerful Facebook is today. Social media has transformed today's communication landscape making it the best tool for businesses to engage their target audience in the easiest, fastest, and most cost efficient way possible!

Now, there's absolutely no denying the power and unbelievable reach of Facebook and social media. With over 400 million regular users and 900 million people with Facebook accounts it is now the best platform for selling your business and marketing your products. Almost every business big and small is using Facebook and social media to build their business and run a more customer friendly service.

If you're still not convinced you need to jump into Facebook to boost your business, here are the top reasons why you should get your hands on your computer and start building your business Facebook page!

**Top Reasons Why Your Business Should be on Facebook**

- **To step-up your customer service.** Facebook will allow you to stay on top of your business 24 hours a day and respond to customer queries and concerns in the fastest way possible. In today's fast paced lifestyle, people want everything to be instant, and so when they need to know something about your product or service they expect a swift reply. Facebook will allow you to respond to every question and concern instantly. Now, you are building a more satisfied market.

- **For better customer interaction.** Facebook allows businesses to hear straight from their customers what they think about a certain product and service. By listening to what customers think about you, this will help you plan on how to improve your business reputation. This is also a great avenue to be open to suggestions from your market.

- **To have better customer engagement opportunities.** Facebook offers new and better opportunities to engage and invite the market to try out your product and service. There are variety of creative and interesting ways to sell your business and get more people interested in your product and service. You can advertise events, promos, contests, an special offers over on Facebook and get the attention you never had with traditional media.

- **To increase your web traffic.** If you're having problems driving people to check out your business website, then Facebook just might be the solution. You can easily post links to your site on your Facebook page and encourage people to click on it to learn more about your product and service. The more traffic you drive to your site, the more opportunities you get to increase your profit.

- **To reach a new world of customers.** With Facebook unimaginable reach your business will be able to tap into new markets you never thought you could reach. The opportunities of engaging people across the world are almost limitless with Facebook.

- **To discover new business leads.** Business leads are all over Facebook. Just try to visit the pages of other business to watch out for possible leads for your business. Just like you, so many other business developers out there are looking to other Facebook business pages to see how they can maximize partnerships.

- **For increased customer retention.** Facebook is a great avenue for conversations with your clients, and the more conversations you share the higher chances of them remembering you and staying with you for long. Facebook makes small, meaningful conversations so much easier; this is what helps build long lasting relationships with customers and even business partners.

- **To build your own presence on-line.** Everyone and everything nowadays are on-line, so if you're not then you're totally missing so much opportunity. The internet and Facebook have now become a very reliable source of information. When looking for reviews on a particular product or service, people run to Facebook for testimonials from consumers themselves. So imagine what you would be missing without a Facebook page!

- **To put a real face into your business.** Facebook allows you to introduce yourself [your company] to your clients so they know who exactly they are doing business with. Posting staff photos while on the job or those happy company event pictures are a great way to put a face and personality to your business. People are naturally more inclined to do business with someone they know in some way.

- **To be identified as cool.** Let's face it, there's nothing more cool today than social network—Facebook and

Twitter. So you would definitely want to be identified among the in crowd with your own Facebook page. Don't be branded as old fashioned and out dated once your interested customers find out you're not even on Facebook... like, where have you been all these years?

No matter where you are in the world, social media now has the power to link you with friends, family, and business partners across great distances and borders. Now, people living halfway around the world thousands of miles away can exchange important information in real time through Facebook and other social networking tools.

Because of the amazing capacity of Facebook, it is now the most promising business tool to engage a much broader audience for the purpose of marketing a product or service. Worldwide, over 90% of all businesses both big and small have built their presence on Facebook and social media.

**How to create a Facebook Page for Your Business**

Now that you know what you can achieve with the help of Facebook, then it's time to get to work and create your own business Facebook Page. The great thing about Facebook is that everything is so user-friendly. Sure, you're no techy person, that's not a problem. With a few easy steps you can definitely navigate your way and create your page in no time.

Unless you've been living under a rock then you can definitely find your way through creating a Facebook profile; now creating a Facebook Page is really no different.

At the sign up page, is a link that will quickly redirect you to creating a Facebook Page. Some people refer to a Facebook Page as a 'Fan Page'—but they are actually the same thing.

**STEP 1:**

You have two choices to begin creating your page. If you're already logged in to our personal Facebook profile, then you can just scroll all the way down the page, until you see the 'Create a Page' link.

Or, you can just go on ahead and paste the link below on your search bar and land on the Create a Page window.

**STEP 2:**
Choose the type of page you need depending on your business. Remember to choose carefully as this will help you as you complete the creation of your page. You may choose between the following:

- Local business or place
- Artist, band, or public figure
- Company, organization, or institution
- Entertainment
- Brand or product
- Cause of community

**STEP 3:**

Fill in the require information on the specific fields. You will notice drop down menus to further narrow down and specify your information. Make sure you list down all information correctly. Make sure your business name is keyed in correctly, because you will not be allowed to edit it after you have earned 100 likes.

Once all information are validated, simply click 'Get Started' and your Facebook Page is live.

**STEP 4:**

To complete your Facebook Page, simply follow three simple steps as shown below.

**First,** you need to upload a photo. Since your promoting your business here, then it's best to upload your business logo. In this way, you are creating recall among your clients. So make sure the image you upload here is the same as the one in your business website and other promotional business materials.

**Second,** you can start inviting you friends and other contacts to visit your page. Facebook will help you do this. You can also share the page in your own Facebook account and like it, so your contacts will be able to see it.

**Third,** now to finish off you will need to upload some basic information about your business. You will only have around 255 characters for this part, so keep it straight to the point. This is one of the most important parts of your page as this is where the public can learn about what you do and the products and services you offer. So think carefully before you fill this part.

That's it! You now have your very own Facebook Page. You will notice that it may still look empty. But that's totally fine, this is now the part where you populate your page with photos, videos, links, and other announcements and information.

**Customizing Your Facebook Page**

Facebook comes with a number of customization tabs to help you create the best page possible. From customizing pictures, to information, color schemes, and even discussion tabs, it's all here! Choose from among the following customization tabs and get started with improving your Facebook Page.

**Info Tab**

Don't wait for your page to reach 100 likes or you won't be able to edit your name. So if you plan to change your page name then do it immediately. But don't worry because your business information can be ever evolving as you go through your business. Keep updating your information every so often so it's always timely.

**Profile Picture Tab**

The best image to upload here is your business logo. Make sure you stay consistent with the business logo you use on-line and off-line. You may upload a jpeg, png, or gif file.

**Wall Tab**

This should be the busiest and most happening part of your Facebook Page. This is where you upload announcements, updates, product promos, and other special offers. Feel free to put regular updates on the field that says 'What's on your mind today?' The more interesting and relevant your updates are the more traffic you will generate on your page. You can also use this field to post links to other relevant sites that people can visit.

**Photos Tab**

Uploading photos will bring life to your Facebook Page. The more photo you upload the more interest you will gain from the public. You can upload as much pictures and albums as you want . For better organization, don't forget to label each album and put captions on them.

# 7. Facebook Marketing

Now that you have your Facebook Page up and running, it's time to get in to Facebook marketing.

'Marketing' has always been known to be a set of activities and methods aimed at creating great value for your clients. Effective marketing will help you get the word out there about your product and service and help you get as much profit as possible.

Facebook Marketing is today's in thing. Much like the traditional marketing, it is all about effectively identifying and understanding your target market and engaging them effectively through various means.

**Facebook Marketing Tips**

Here are a few quick tips to help you market your product through Facebook more effectively. Social media is the most interactive platform of communication today, so you need to arm yourself with a few tricks so you can keep up with the market and stay at par with the best pages out there.

**1. Sync your blog with your Facebook Page**

To make sure your business website is in sync with your Facebook Page, upload your blog on the page. Every time you enter a new blog entry the same thing will appear on your Facebook Page. This allows you to have interactive content updated regularly. Look for the 'Import an External Blog' tab on your page and fill out the necessary fields.

**2. Create compelling content**

The type of content you post can make or break your business. One of the best ways to engage your audience more effectively is by using compelling and clear call to action lines. You may use lines like 'Like us now!', 'Share the page with your friends', or 'Support this cause by liking us'.

### 3. Add pages on your Favorites

You have total freedom to add pages as your Favorite. When you do, you can likewise ask other business pages to add yours as their Favorite, too! By doing this you are endorsing other pages to your network and they're doing the same to you.

### 4. Provide quick access to your Facebook Page

As we have been repeating over and over, millions of people are on Facebook every day. So it will do your business good to have a quick link from your official business website that directly pushes to your Facebook page. Don't give your customers a hard time finding you.

### 5. Utilize aps and tabs
There are countless tabs and apps available for your Facebook page; there are aps for newsletters, news updates, videos, blogs and so many more. Try to maximize this to share more information about your business and products. You will be amazed at how useful these apps can turn out to be.

### 6. Embed Youtube videos on your Facebook Page

Make your page so much more interesting with the use of videos. Users are naturally more inclined to check out moving images. With the help of Youtube, uploading videos on your page is so easy

### 7. Ask your own fans to spread the word

Facebook allows you to add an 'Invite your Friends' box to your page that will help your fans spread the word about you to their own friends! Remember that in Facebook marketing you need a clear strategy on how to engage and reach as many people as possible.

**Common Facebook Marketing Mistakes**

After learning some key tips to effectively market your business using Facebook, it would be best to familiarize yourself with common mistakes many businesses commit in their effort to maximize Facebook to their advantage.

Some business developers become too excited about populating their page that they end up committing too many mistakes in the process. Many of these common mistakes are really avoidable, so it's best to go over these items and try to remind yourself not to fall prey to them. Remember even the smallest mistakes can mean huge effects to your product and services.

• Not giving importance to the profile page of your business. This is where potential customers will learn key information about your products and services, so make sure you fill it out properly and completely. It should contain essential information about your business like your contact details, business hours, and links to your official business website.

• Don't slack off and leave some fields incomplete, this little mistake could mean potential clients an business partners lost.

• Focusing on quantity rather than quality. When posting content, remember that quality is more important than quantity. Don't make the mistake of over posting stuff and bombarding your audience with too much information more than they need and will appreciate. You want your market to be excited about what you will post next and look forward to quality content from you. So make sure to schedule content posting carefully so that you maximize the page properly.

• Using weird cover photos. Never use illegal photos for your cover- or even photos that are grabbed. The cover photo must speak well of your product and service. You should also update your cover photo every once in a while just to give it a fresh look. But make sure your photos are interesting and communicate your brand.

• Posting content that is as long as a novel. Try to avoid posts that are way too long. Readers will most like scroll past your post if it readily appears too long. Keep your word count between 100-250 words, anything longer could be an instant turn off to readers.

• To draw more conversations and comments on your posts, try to include open ended questions that will make them think and share what they think. Remember getting people to click 'like' on your posts is not enough, what you want is to get people to become interested enough to share their own views. So try to make your posts as creative as possible.

• Becoming insignificant. If your product or service is about pastries then make sure you post only relevant, significant information connected to your business. Don't post stuff just because you think it's cool, remember your Facebook Page should mirror your business and the experience you wish to impart to your customers. So don't get caught with far-fetched, insignificant photos or blog posts.

- On the other hand, posting timely content related to your business is the best way to draw attention to your product or service.

- Ignoring useful Facebook data. Pay attention to Facebook insights. Never ignore what the numbers and charts say about your Facebook marketing. These are relevant information you need to take and consider to help you improve the way you market your business. The effectivity of social media marketing may be harder to measure as compared to traditional media, which makes these insights and charts all the more important.

- Sit with your team and try to interpret what these insights say, and draw out concrete plans to do better each month. Then keep assessing how you improve month after month.

## Writing Effective Content for Your Business Page

A whole lot of the success of Facebook marketing rests on effective content management. No matter how great your page looks like or how much time you spend on packing it with apps, videos, and photos, if you fall flat on content then no one will really ever take you or your business seriously. Well written content is the backbone of effective customer engagement and marketing. What you say on Facebook will either capture audience attention or drive them away; you can be so interesting and cool that people will want to be identified with your brand or you can come off as super boring that no one will really care what you have to say.

Facebook and social media are amazing tools to reach the widest possible market for your product and service, imagine how many people log in everyday and are potential customers. It would be a shame not to be able to engage the properly when they're just actually there ready to listen to good content.

So before you write anything or post anything think carefully on how it will impact your audience. View it as an opportunity to win customers over and make new acquaintances. This can be your business' chance for greatness so make sure you do it right.

Here are some very useful tips to help you generate content that will capture people's attention and interest, and build your presence in the huge world of social media. There are so many different voices out there competing against yours, so you need to make sure yours is heard the loudest.

- Know your audience, and know them well. This is the first step to even planning what to tell them and what to talk about with them. Understand their demographics and interests, and then speak their language.

- Boring has no place in the social media world. Either people totally browse past your message or they never even know you were there. Yes, Facebook is where the fun and cool guys go to connect to the world, so really, boring has no place there.

- Quit using your business jargons! Stop sounding like a college science professor when posting content. Write something simple and conversational. Write as if you're talking to a friend face to face. Use regular day-to-day language. Remember you're not there to impress them with your words.

- Keep your words short and sweet. The way to go in social media is to share brief, straight to the point one-liners. Keep each post and comment to a minimum. If you must post longer content then make sure to break them up to shorter paragraphs, use headers, and bullet lists to allow some breathing space for the eyes. You will be surprised at how many people will respond and like your post.

•       Don't take things too seriously when posting stuff in Facebook. Have fun with it. Loosen up. You don't need to make fun of people or your business, just try to creatively inject some humor and use a less serious tone when writing. People go to Facebook to have fun, relax, and unwind from a stressful day… so do your fans a favor and don't give them anymore stress with your lecture.

•       Images are the best way to drive a message. Would you rather read an entire story of 1,000 words or stare at an amazing photo and a 50-word caption that tells the story? It's a no brainer. Choose creative images over long blocks of text and your fans will love you.

•       Try to give educational information and sound advice when appropriate. We all like learning new things. But remember all the other rules still apply. Write briefly and don't bore them to death. And try to use images if necessary.

•       If you have interesting stories to share about your business' humble beginnings then share it on your page. Try to inject pieces of it every once in a while when appropriate. People like hearing real stories that put a human touch to your product and service.

•       Never share and post anything that you yourself won't waste time reading. Remember, your fans re also regular people just like you.

**Facebook's Not-so-secret Recipe to Success**

When Mark Zuckerberg was creating the Facebook project in his dorm room, he never thought it would be this huge! Sure it was a great idea that showed promise... but to think it would be worth billions someday was nowhere near his mind.

At that time there were other social networking sites in existence, but Facebook just managed to get ahead of them all and stay ahead. So what could be the secret to Zuckerberg's success? How did he take an idea and turn it into something that revolutionized the world?

Here a few secrets to Facebook's success that could very well be applied to our own business.

### Speed

Great ideas don't always come by, but when they do you need to act on it fast. Zuckerberg built on his Facebook idea the very moment he had the idea. Never mind doing lengthy researches, conducting interviews, or assembling focus groups... he did not waste time and went to work immediately. In a few weeks, the social networking site that would affect millions of people was created.

### Simplicity is key

Often times we need to remind our self not to overdo things. Products and services that come out too complex for anyone to really understand and appreciate will never really make it big. Keep it simple, effective, and easy to use.

When then called 'thefacebook' came out, it was so simple that anyone could operate and appreciate, there were no frills. People just went on and enjoyed the service! And that was how word spread about its functionality and creativity.

### Great idea + effective execution = success

You may have heard people say that 'ideas are a dime a dozen'. We all get great ideas at some point in our life, but what spells success from failure is the way we execute our ideas. Never stop at just your brilliant idea, you need to take it a step further and execute it. Take that leap of faith and work towards making it happen. If Zuckerberg had stopped with just his idea, then Facebook would never have been born.

### Focus on building the product and service

Sure you want to earn money, what businessman doesn't. But make sure you invest well on building great customer service and products that will satisfy the market. While you want to get profit, remind yourself that your main purpose is to give your customers a great experience with your product.

In the early days of Facebook, Zuckerberg refused opportunities from advertisers for the simple reason that he wanted the site to remain cool for his users, and placing ads weren't cool enough.

### Keep innovating

Take the challenge of innovating new products and services based on what you think your market will enjoy. You don't always need to go through the lengths of market research and interviews, listen to your intuition, if you think your market will like it then go on right ahead. To strike a balance, make sure you're ready to pull out when it doesn't seem to work.

In the case of Facebook, Zuckerberg always tried to figure out what the market wanted and innovated something for them. If it worked then he continued, but if it did not then he pulled back.

### Learn from the best

In running your business, never assume to know everything. Business development is a continuous learning process. Make a list of the people you look up to and learn from them. There's always something new to learn from the business, so try to keep improving on your craft.

Zuckerberg wasn't a CEO by profession; his background was with computer programming. But faced with the need to run his business, he learned as much as he could to be a worthy CEO. He had peope he looked up to help mentor him—big names like Steve Jobs and Peter Thiel. Soon, he knew the ropes of running Facebook with more confidence.

### Study your competition

Getting into business is like gearing up for battle. Make sure you arm yourself with knowledge to tacke your competitors and draw a game plan on how to get ahead of them. Study how other players in the market work and what could possibly kill your business. Make sure you know their advantage over yours and begin working on how to conquer that.

When Facebook entered there were other social networking sites existing, but Zuckerberg knew what could possibly kill his idea, he studied the competition and came in ready for battle. Now, all his competitors are gone while Facebook is still well on its way to the top.

### Love what you do

You will never last doing anything that you don't love. Always treat your business as an opportunity to live out your passions. Love every bit of what you do and allow it to reflect in your services and the way you run your business. Never go into business for the sake of making money, because you will soon find yourself exhausted. Just go out there and love what you do!

There is absolutely no doubt that Zuckerberg was in love with the very idea of Facebook. From the very first days he began creating the site, he poured in so much passion into it. And that could very well be his edge over the other networking sites that were ever built.

Always remember that success is not limited to a Mark Zuckerberg. Anyone can achieve the same success and even more, all it takes is a great balance of the essential elements mentioned above. So go out there and aim for success.

# 8. Creating Your Facebook Marketing Plan

Effective planning is key in any undertaking. A well thought out plan is half the battle, now all that's left is executing the plan strategically and you're on your way to success! Similar to building a house, the builders work based on a blueprint; in the same way you and your team must have a Facebook marketing plan structured perfectly in place to guide you as you maximize social media to promote and sell your business.

Never underestimate the importance of a marketing plan, this will help your team to work cohesively towards a united goal and not work aimlessly without achieving anything. When people work together guided by a plan then they have better chances of succeeding.

**Essential Elements for Creating a Marketing Plan**

Below are the essential elements you need to draw out as you create your marketing plan.

**Determine your objectives**

Before anything else you need to draw out what your objectives are for your Facebook Page. Is your page for displaying and selling your products? Are you starting an advocacy campaign for a social issue? Do you just want to drive traffic to your site through Facebook? Ask yourself 'why do I want to be on social media and what is my main goal for being on Facebook?

Whatever your objectives are it's up to you, but make sure you decide on some clear and achievable objectives before you set out to go full blast on your marketing plans. Then, don't forget to set a timeframe between which you will see if you have achieved your objectives.

**Determine your target audience**

This is the most important step after you've finalized your objectives. For you to be able to be effective in anything you do from here on, you need to know who you are talking to. Ask yourself 'who do I want to reach with my business and message?' Try to be as specific as possible with your target audience; narrow them down to as specific as possible. What is their age? Gender? Are they from the working class? What is their income range? Try to answer key questions to help you arrive at your intended target market.

Only after you have successfully identified your target market will you appreciate how easy all the other next steps are. Because once you get this right, then all other elements will be guided.

**Strategize your content**

Now, to be able to achieve the objectives you have set for the specific audience you have selected you need to carefully plan out your content and how you will post it—this will determine how effective you can achieve your objectives.

There are four types of content people use to maximize their use of Facebook:

- Facebook Polls
- Pictures
- Videos
- Links to other pages

By utilizing these content properly your site will begin to generate meaningful and interesting conversations. The more interactions you generate the more visits and likes your page will receive. You also need to ask yourself what kind of content can best reach your target audience. What type of message will your market find interesting enough to talk about and share to their networks.

**Create a content calendar**

Make a table to schedule the content you will upload daily, weekly, and even monthly. You may begin with a 3-month calendar of content you can follow. You can start with January- March. Think back on the objectives you have set and revisit the target market you identified, from here decide on what content you should upload to achieve your goals.

You can also consider the general calendar-events specific to a given month, like New Year in January, Valentine's in February and so on. Remember you need to stay current, so if people are talking about the New Year then your content must be timely and relevant. Don't worry about trying to connect it with your business, just be creative with it and your market will appreciate it.

Having a content plan will help you generate continuous and interesting messages that will generate conversations between your network and best market your business. Before your content plan ends, make sure to plan for the next succeeding months.

**Manage your page**

Monitor your page daily. Regardless how often you have scheduled your content uploads, you need to monitor your page daily. Go over your newsfeeds and check for comments, interesting conversation threads, questions, and any other activity going on that you may be able to maximize.

Before the day ends, monitor any page activity that may need your attention. Make sure you follow the content plan you have set to keep your page interesting and to have better chances of achieving your objectives at the end of the timeframe you set.

## Measure results

There are simple ways of measuring the effectiveness of your Facebook marketing plan. Do this at the middle of the marketing plan timeframe and at the end to see how good or bad you performed. Facebook offers quick insights in a tab found under interactions. Here, you can see the posts you made and the feedback it received from your fans. *See sample below.*

Based on your objectives you can also draw out specific metrics to measure your success. If your first objective is to 'Create Awareness' then you may want to check out how many new Facebook fans you have garnered from the marketing plan you followed. Remember to be realistic with the metrics you will use to measure; stick with ideas that are measurable, like the number of likes, amount of sales, email sign-ups, new subscribers to your newsletter, etc. Draw out measurable items that will help you asses each strategy or objective you have set.

Creating your marketing plan and executing it are tricky methods but once you are able to carry them out effectively then the fruits of your labor will be sweet! With a little hard work and consistency your marketing plan is sure to succeed.

## Go Viral on Facebook with a Few Easy Tips

Every business wants to have more followers, more likes, more fans, more views, more traffic... we all want our business pages to be more popular than the rest. Imagine if you could get a single post on your business page to be seen by millions and interacted upon by millions? You would be saving huge amounts of money while building your name.

Every time you post something on your Facebook page your objective is to get the most attention to it as possible and have people like it, talk about it, share it to their friends, and repost it on their own Facebook pages and accounts—this is how you go viral! Just like a virus, you want your content to spread uncontrollably across groups and places, until as much people are infected by you and your content.

But with millions of information shared and exchanged every single day over Facebook and social media it's not easy at all to go viral. For you to be noticed you need to rise above all the social media noise and be heard. Your message needs to be so much more interesting and compelling for people to pick it up amongst all the virtual clutter. Though this is hard, it is definitely not impossible. Here are a few tips and tricks that just might take you viral in no time.

### Build your following

Interestingly you don't need millions of followers to go viral. But you can turn your 1,000 followers to 1 million once you do. Try to build a conservative number of loyal 'fans' on your page; create meaningful interactions with the because this will be the foundation of going viral one day. Imagine if each of your 1,000 warm followers will share your content to 1,000 more of their own friends? Imagine the reach you can have with a single message. So, nurture what network you now have because they are the ones who will help you go viral.

### Stay current and trendy

No one will ever like or share content that's old news. But if you try to stay current then you have better chances of getting viewed because people are searching for current news on Google and other similar sites; who knows they just might land on your page.

If you're running a business page, don't think that current events and new trends are irrelevant to your product and service. You just need to be creative and find ways to link the news to your page. There are ways to maximize current news to draw attention to your page.

## Maximize keywords and tags

Never underestimate the power of keywords and tags; using these strategically can draw the line between being searchable and viewed to never having a single person find you. Remember that when people search for topics and content they use keywords, so if you have these keywords embedded all throughout your content— on the title, subheadings, and the main text. Often times, just using the right words will make a noticeable difference in the number of views you get.

## Throw a contest

Contests are a sure way of getting attention. If you can't seem to get a good number of people to take notice of your content, then try starting a contest. Just make sure to make the rules and details very simple and interesting. Remember you're doing this mainly to gather fans and not to educate people. Again, try to be current and trendy with the contest idea and make sure you consider your target market and what will interest them. A really cool, fun game can just get you the fans you have been dreaming of.

## Share something on a random act of kindness

This one never fails. Catching everyday people doing good in this day and age when people are just growing more and more apathetic is a surefire way to go viral. People like hearing about inspiring stories and people who go out of their way to be a hero to someone in need. Share content like this and you just might get a million thumbs up from the virtual world. Trust me, people still like hearing good news.

### Draw attention on a social issue

Sharing content about issues relevant to the general public more often than not generates attention. Calling out a company or business for violation of human rights or for poor customer service is also a great way to get noticed and possibly go viral. This does not mean to destroy other people and their business, but simply to draw attention to the negativity that the society is beginning to get used to with the objective of helping correct it.

### Opt for visuals rather than text blocks

It is quite obvious that people will always find good pictures and videos way more interesting than a block of text that they have to read over just to appreciate. A good visual material communicates so much more than a story can at a single glance. So, if you want to catch attention and be shared over social media, then go for videos and photos.

### Be exciting

No body picks up on anything boring. To actually go viral you need offer something that has never been done before; if people come across something new this will definitely stir excitement enough for your content and your page to be liked, shared, and visited… and then you begin going viral.

Facebook has allowed businesses to listen to what their customers need so they can better satisfy their needs and give them a better brand experience. Since everyone's on Facebook it has also helped the market stay updated with their latest offers, promos, products, and events. Now, when you want to know anything about a certain product all you need to do is to check them out on Facebook and all you need to know about them is there!

**Get More Fans on Your Page**

While individuals are all going crazy over Facebook, business groups are not being left out. What started out as a simple networking tool has now evolved into a marketing, advertising, and even fundraising tool for so many businesses both big and small. Facebook's capacity to reach millions with just a single post and communicate a message to them while spending so little has made it a very efficient method for business developers to build their product and brand.

Once you create a Facebook page it's entirely up to you to utilize and maximize it for your business— making Facebook marketing today's in thing. Since there are over 900 million people on Facebook it just makes perfect sense to maximize this platform to reach the widest market possible. And with Facebook there are no monthly fees to use it; it's just all up to you to strategize the way you interact with your market and get more fans!

To make sure you're on the bandwagon on the road to success, here are a few tips to help you get more fans viewing, liking, and talking about your page.

**Always make the effort to educate, inspire, and entertain**

Try to delight your audiences with the stuff you post. To increase your likes, you will need to convert casual visitors to fans by giving them reason to take interest in the content you post enough for them to actually hit 'like'. If you're content is downright boring, then every visitor will definitely head out without browsing over the rest of your message.

**Take the risk of spending on advertising your page**

If you think about it, all your brilliant content will be useless if no one really sees it. And to advertise your page will boost your exposure and jumpstart your fan growth. The trick is to get the word out to where the right people are, those who you really target. Once you do this successfully, then you know have a head start and better chances of building more and more fans.

**Optimize your page for mobile convenience**

Let's face it, we're in the generation where people are always in a rush, running around from one meeting to the next, travelling across the world to do business, and so on. With that said, research has proven that over 70% of all Facebook users log on through their mobile devices will on the run. Mobile Facebook application is now the in thing. So to help your audience enjoy your page and its content on their mobile device, make sure to post lightweight stuff like easy to load images and quick poll questions. Avoid heavy videos that take forever to load completely. Once they find your content interesting, all it takes is for them to hit 'like' on their mobile device and you automatically get a new fan!

**Set off that viral loop of people liking your**

This is best done through interesting content that people will share to their friends, and then their friends will share to their friends… and so on. You need to keep your fans talking about you, your product, your great service, a new promo, an inspiring true story, an amazing photo… whatever it is, people need to constantly be talking about you.

**Try giveaways**

Let's be honest, who doesn't want to receive free stuff? We all do. And with the slightest chance of winning something, we all readily jump on it. So to get more fans on your page, try throwing a raffle where each potential fan has an easy chance of winning by just doing something simple. Don't forget to ask them to like your page while you're at it. To keep costs low, give out your own product samples. This has been a tried and tested strategy by so many other businesses on Facebook.

**Get bloggers to talk about your business**

These influential people have great clout and can do wonders for your Facebook page. Look for the best group of bloggers that matches your product and service perfectly. Build a relationship with them, and then invite them to try your product and get involved in your network. Once these bloggers start talking about your business and endorsing you fans will start pouring in!

**Work with the big ones**

Go over Facebook and find other pages similar to yours—either they have a similar business or a similar social objective. Pay close attention to those with a lot of fans. Since you generally share the same objectives, write them and ask for the possibility of them posting your link on their page. You can also work on an ex-deal with them, by offering a product or service in exchange. Being seen and even endorsed in pages with a lot of following, will surely give you the boost of fans you need.

The past decade has seen a steady increase in the number of people using Facebook. They project to hit the 1 billion mark by 2012, and it really doesn't seem like an impossibility to reach the mark by the remaining months of 2012. The Facebook craze doesn't seem to show signs of dying down any time soon, so many people still can't seem to get enough of social media. And with so many new techy gadgets on the rise to support social media use, then we'll surely see more people jumping onto the bandwagon.

# 9. Conclusion

When the internet hit its highest point years ago it totally changed the course of how people did business, how learning institutions imparted knowledge, and practically how every known system worked. Everything was now computerized, and centralized through the internet; people communicated across great distances with ease, information was shared in as easy as a click of a button.

And then social media went full blast over the recent years, and it was like everything went into overdrive—people were connected through virtual communities 24/7, news was disseminated as fast as it happens, users had the freedom of generating content themselves and sharing it to the world. All these were unimaginable decades ago.

There is no denying the huge role of Facebook in revolutionizing the way people communicated and interacted with the world. It wasn't the first social media tool out there, but it did what the others couldn't and the public loved it!

Today, it would be impossible to find someone who didn't know someone who had a Facebook account. From as young as grade school kids to as old as grandparents, they're all in Facebook. Whether you're running a business page or just posting personal stuff for your family, Facebook remains the best platform out there. It's free, it's readily available, it's so fun to use, and it connect you to the world.

As you utilize Facebook to your advantage, don't forget to be a responsible user. In as much as you want to engage the most number of people possible you need to be very respectful of other people. Be honest with the content you share, be sensitive to others making sure you do not upload and share offensive material.

Have fun and be strategic with Facebook and social media but never forget to respect others.

Despite all the controversy surrounding Mark Zuckerberg's creation of Facebook, at the end of the day he still remains to be a huge inspiration to so many people out there. No matter how seemingly small or simple your ideas are if you just put your heart into it and take that leap of faith then you are bound to succeed. Imagine if Zuckerberg never took that challenge of pursuing his ideas... we would be missing out on something so great. So just get out there and put your ideas into work.